Crispus Attucks

Heroes of the American Revolution

★

I AM I NOT A MAN AND A BROTHER?

Don McLeese

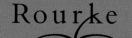
Rourke
Publishing LLC
Vero Beach, Florida 32964

www.rourkepublishing.com

PHOTO CREDITS: Covers, Pages 12, 14, 28 ©Getty Images; Pages 5, 19, 20, 23, 24 ©North Wind Picture Archives; Title page, Pages 6, 8, 9, 10, 16, 26, 27 from the Library of Congress

Title page: *An anti-slavery symbol appeals for an end to slavery.*

Editor: Frank Sloan

Cover and page design by Nicola Stratford

Library of Congress Cataloging-in-Publication Data

McLeese, Don.
 Crispus Attucks / Don McLeese.
    p. cm. -- (Heroes of the American Revolution)
 Includes bibliographical references (p.   ) and index.
 ISBN 1-59515-218-0
 1. Attucks, Crispus, d. 1770--Juvenile literature. 2. African Americans--
Biography--Juvenile literature. 3. Revolutionaries--Massachusetts--Boston--
Biography--Juvenile literature. 4. Boston Massacre, 1770--Juvenile literature. 5.
Attucks, Crispus, d. 1770. I. Title. II. Series: McLeese, Don. Heroes of the
American Revolution.
 E185.97.A86M39 2004
 973.3'113'092--dc22

                        2004007608

Printed in the USA

w/w

Table of Contents

★

He Died for His Country

★

Of all the American heroes of the Revolutionary War era, we know the least about Crispus Attucks. He didn't become famous until after his death. He was the first man killed by the British in the war that became known as the American Revolution.

On March 5, 1770, British soldiers in Boston, Massachusetts, killed Crispus Attucks and four other Americans. This battle between Americans and British soldiers became known as the Boston **Massacre**. Americans who thought this land should no longer be ruled by England said that the deaths of Crispus Attucks and the others showed how bad the British were. Lots of other Americans decided to follow the example of Crispus and fight the British.

We remember Crispus Attucks as a brave man who gave his life so that a new country could be born: the United States of America.

British soldiers shoot at local residents during the Boston Massacre.

Slaves crowd on board a ship as it leaves Africa.

Son of a Slave

★

Crispus's father was named Prince Yonger. He came from Africa, where he was captured and taken to America. After the ship carrying him arrived in Massachusetts, he was sold as a **slave**.

Crispus's mother was named Nancy Attucks. She was a **Native American** from the Natick tribe.

Most **historians** think that Crispus Attucks was born in 1723, in the colony of Massachusetts.

SLAVERY

Today, countries throughout the world know that slavery is wrong, that one person shouldn't be allowed to own another person. Slavery was outlawed in the United States in 1863, when the **Emancipation** Proclamation set all slaves free.

~

Part of the reason we know so little about Crispus's life is that he was the son of a slave. Later, he became a slave himself. Back then, white people who came from Europe considered themselves better than black people who came from Africa. According to the laws in America at that time, white people could own black people and make them work hard without giving them any money. These people who were owned were called slaves.

Abraham Lincoln sits at the left as the Emancipation Proclamation is first read.

An African is inspected just before he is sold.

Early Years a Mystery

★

Because little attention was paid to recording the facts of an African-American's life in those days, we don't know much about the boyhood of Crispus. We don't know which family owned his father, so we're not sure where Crispus grew up. We know that Crispus himself became a slave. Sons of slaves were considered **property** rather than being free. He was owned by William Brown of Framingham, in the **colony** of Massachusetts.

A Valuable Slave

★

Crispus must have been a very smart slave. He made money by doing business with white men, selling them horses and cattle. He saved some of this money in the hope that he could buy his freedom from William Brown. But because he also made money for his owner by selling horses, William Brown said that Crispus was too important and refused to let him go.

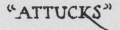

"ATTUCKS"

In the Native American language of Crispus's mother, the word "attucks" means "deer."

～

A portrait of Crispus Attucks

A whaling ship at sea

Escape!

★

In 1750, when he was 27 years old, Crispus Attucks ran away from William Brown. We know this because Brown put a notice in the Boston newspaper describing his slave:

"A **mulatto** fellow, about 27 years of age, named Crispus, 6 feet and 2 inches high, short curl'd hair." In the notice, Brown asked for Crispus back and said that anyone helping the slave would be breaking the law.

But Crispus was too smart to get caught. He seemed to disappear. Some say that he took a job on a ship that sailed the ocean to catch whales. Nothing was heard about Crispus for 20 years.

WHALING SHIPS

Working at sea on a whaling ship was very hard. The ships would be away from land for months at a time.

~

Fugitive slaves were often shot if they were caught.

Off to Sea

★

Later, it was learned that Crispus Attucks had spent much of his time after running away as a sailor. He went to Boston and worked on ships that were trying to catch whales. Because he was away at sea for much of the time, it was harder for William Brown to find him and bring him back to slavery. William Brown never got his slave back, and Crispus lived as a free man.

FUGITIVE

An escaped slave was called a "fugitive," which means someone who is running away from the law.

~

Back to Boston

★

In the fall of 1769, Crispus Attucks decided to leave the sea and return to live in Boston. It had been almost 20 years since his escape, and no one was looking for him any longer. Attucks found work making ropes. It was hard to be a rope maker, but it was better than being a slave. And it was a good change for him to live on land after spending so much time sailing the seas.

A view of Boston in the late 1700s

King George III of England

Battling the British

★

Because America was still ruled by Britain at the time, there were British soldiers in Boston. Many Americans thought they shouldn't be ruled by another country across the ocean, that America should be its own country with its own laws. The people didn't want to obey the king of England. They wanted to elect their own leaders. They wanted a **democracy**, where every voter would help decide who the leader would be and who would make the laws.

DEMOCRACY

At the time, most countries were ruled by kings who were born to the job rather than elected to it. America wanted to try a new form of government called democracy, where the people would decide who their rulers would be.

~

Because British soldiers served the government and king of England, there were sometimes arguments or even fights between the soldiers and the Americans living in Boston. Some of the British soldiers also took jobs to make more money. These were jobs that people such as Crispus Attucks felt Americans should have. There was often trouble between the British soldiers and the Americans living in Boston.

British troops enter Boston to enforce taxation on the natives.

A colonial boy taunts a British soldier.

The Trouble Gets Worse

★

In February of 1770, the trouble between British soldiers and Americans turned more serious. A Boston boy had been making fun of the soldiers. Perhaps he had even thrown things at them. A British soldier got mad and shot at the boy with his gun. This made many of the Americans in Boston very angry. Whatever the boy had done, he didn't deserve to be shot by the British.

Crispus Attucks made a speech in Boston. He said that the Americans needed to fight the British in order to be free.

Not long afterward, there was a bigger fight between British soldiers and Boston rope makers on March 2, 1770. Such fights were between Americans who wanted the freedom to start their own country and soldiers who were loyal to the king of England. These fights led to the American Revolution. As a former slave, Crispus Attucks was one of the biggest believers in freedom for every American.

The Boston Massacre

SAMUEL ADAMS

Adams was a leader in American independence, but he said Americans should only fight the British if all else failed. The Boston Massacre showed that Americans would need to fight if they wanted their freedom.

On March 5, 1770, an American leader named Samuel Adams called for American workers to protest against the British soldiers. He said that America shouldn't be ruled by Britain. America should become its own country. And everyone who agreed should follow him.

Crispus Attucks was one of the first to follow Adams. A group of about 40 or 50 Americans went toward the British soldiers. Some carried sticks or clubs as weapons. A few even had snowballs.

The British felt they were under attack, so they started firing their guns. Since Attucks was at the front, he was the first to die. Four more Americans were shot to death by the British that day. The event became known as the Boston Massacre.

A scene of the Boston Massacre, in which Attucks was killed

The colonists tried to fight back, but they were no match for the British soldiers.

A Hero in Death

★

Though few people knew Crispus Attucks's name when he was alive, in death he became a famous hero. He was the first to die in the Boston Massacre, the first to die for his country in the Revolutionary War. As a slave, he wasn't even allowed to have his freedom in America, but he still thought that this country was worth fighting for.

In 1888, Boston celebrated him with the Crispus Attucks Monument, a statue that still stands in Boston Common. In 1998, President Bill Clinton honored Crispus Attucks and others with the Black Patriots Coin Law, with the coin issued on the 275th anniversary of the birth of Crispus Attucks.

Time Line

1723 ★ Crispus is born.

1750 ★ Crispus runs away from William Brown.

1769 ★ Crispus leaves the sea and returns to Boston.

1770 ★ There is a fight between British soldiers and Boston rope makers.

1770 ★ Samuel Adams calls for American workers to protest against the British, and Crispus Attucks is killed in the Boston Massacre.

1998 ★ President Clinton honors Crispus Attucks on the 275th anniversary of his birth.

Glossary

colony (KOL ih nee) — a territory ruled by another country

democracy (di MOK ruh see) — government by the people, who vote to elect their leaders

emancipation (ih MAN suh PAY shun) — setting free

historians (his TOR ee anz) — people who are experts in the study of history

massacre (MAS ih kur) — a violent attack that results in a number of deaths

mulatto (muh LAT oh) — someone born to parents of different races

Native American (NAYT iv uh MER uh kun) — a member of the tribes (sometimes called "Indians") who lived in North America before explorers from Europe came here

property (PROP urt ee) — something belonging to someone

slave (SLAYV) — a person owned by another person

Index

Further Reading

Beier, Anne. *Crispus Attucks: Hero of the Boston Massacre.* The Rosen
   Publishing Group, Incorporated, 2003.

Buckley, Gail Lumet. *American Patriots: A Young People's Edition: The Story
   of Blacks in the Military from the Revolution to Desert Storm.* Crown
   Books for Young Readers, 2003.

Mattern, Joanne. *Cost of Freedom: Crispus Attucks and the Boston Massacre.*
   The Rosen Publishing Group, Incorporated, 2004.

Websites to Visit

http://www.africawithin.com/bios/crispus_attucks.htm

http://search.eb.com/blackhistory/micro/40/36.html

http://www.bridgew.edu/HOBA/Inductees/Attucks.htm

About the Author

Don McLeese is an award-winning journalist whose work has appeared in many
newspapers and magazines. He earned his M.A. degree in English from the University
of Chicago, taught feature writing at the University of Texas and has frequently
contributed to the World Book Encyclopedia. He lives with his wife and two daughters
in West Des Moines, Iowa.